Inside the NFL

THE
NEW ORLEANS
SAINTS

B O B   I T A L I A
ABDO & Daughters

Published by Abdo & Daughters, 4940 Viking Drive, Suite 622, Edina, Minnesota 55435.

Copyright © 1996 by Abdo Consulting Group, Inc., Pentagon Tower, P.O. Box 36036, Minneapolis, Minnesota 55435 USA. International copyrights reserved in all countries. No part of this book may be reproduced in any form without written permission from the publisher.

Printed in the United States.

Cover Photo credit: Wide World Photos / Allsport
Interior Photo credits: Wide World Photos

Edited by Kal Gronvall

Library of Congress Cataloging-in-Publication Data

Italia, Bob, 1955—
      The New Orleans Saints/Bob Italia
           p. cm. -- (Inside the NFL)
      Includes index.
      Summary: Covers the history of and the key players for the team that has never made it past the first round of the playoffs in the NFC West.
      ISBN 1-56239-532-7
      1. New Orleans Saints (Football team) -- Juvenile literature. [1. New Orleans Saints (Football team)] I. Title. II. Series:
      Italia, Bob, 1955— Inside the NFL.
      GV956.N366I83 1996
      796.332'64'0976335--dc20   95-40360
                                                                  CIP
                                                                    AC

CONTENTS

From Aints to Saints

For many years, the New Orleans Saints were known for their losing tradition. Fans once wore paper bags at home games and called their team the "Aints." But then the team acquired quarterback Bobby Hebert while developing an All-Star linebacking corps. Suddenly, the Aints were Saints, and they marched through opponent after opponent.

Quarterback Richard Todd scrambles from defensive pursuit.

In the 1980s, the Saints won the tough NFC (National Football Conference) West and had the NFL's (National Football League's) best defense. But New Orleans could never put their top-rated defense to use in the playoffs and advance past the first round. Frustrated, management traded away Hebert and the once-impenetrable defensive corps.

These days, New Orleans is in search of another leader who can take them back to the top of the NFC West. Should the defense recover from its current doldrums, the Saints may challenge the NFL's elite teams for the Super Bowl championship.

**Opposite page:
Chuck Muncie breaks away
for a gain against Tampa Bay.**

Beginnings

On November 1, 1967, New Orleans received news from NFL commissioner Pete Rozelle that the city had been given an NFL expansion franchise. John Mecom, a 29-year-old businessman from Houston, Texas, bought the franchise for $8.5 million. He named his team the Saints, after the famous New Orleans jazz song, "When the Saints Go Marchin' In."

The New Orleans Saints first coach Tom Fears (right) and the team owner John Mecom.

Mecom was the NFL's youngest club owner, and he often involved himself with the day-to-day operations of the team. Early in 1967, Mecom hired Tom Fears as the team's first head coach.

Fears had plenty of NFL experience. He had been a member of the 1951 Los Angeles Rams' NFL championship team, and held a Rams' team and NFL record for the most receptions (18) in a single game. Fears had also been an assistant to the legendary Vince Lombardi, the head coach of the Green Bay Packers.

Fears was the ideal candidate to develop a young expansion team. He worked his players hard in training camp. Veterans and rookies often complained about how hard the practices were. But as he had learned from Lombardi, hard work and discipline often translated into championships.

But without talented players, all the hard work would not pay off. Fortunately for Fears, he had some talent with which to work. Quarterback Bill Kilmer led the Saints to one of the NFL's best records for an expansion club.

Kilmer had been traded by the San Francisco 49ers. He thought his football career was over. But Coach Fears gave him another chance.

Kilmer often passed to wide receiver Dan Abramowicz. Abramowicz had been a seventeenth-round draft pick and would one day hold the Saints' career records in pass receiving and touchdowns. He quickly became a key player in the Saints' offense, and was known for his pass-catching ability.

Tom Dempsey
and the Kick

Another star player was placekicker Tom Dempsey. He made NFL history in a game against the Detroit Lions on November 8, 1970. Dempsey entered the game with only two seconds remaining. The Saints had the ball on their own 45-yard line, and trailed Detroit by one point. New head coach J. D. Roberts sent Dempsey in to attempt a 63-yard field goal. The crowd was silent. Though Dempsey had a strong leg, the NFL field goal record was 56 yards.

Dempsey was up to the challenge. He had succeeded in football despite being disabled. Dempsey had been born without a right hand and with only half a right foot. Teased by his peers, he was determined to show his athletic abilities. He played tackle for his high school football team, and was good enough to sign to a professional contract while in junior college.

Quarterback Billy Kilmer.

Holder Joe Scarpati took the snap and watched as Dempsey made his usual two-and-a-half-step run at the ball. Detroit's All-Pro lineman Alex Karras had a shot at blocking the kick, but he was too stunned to give it his best effort.

Dempsey's mallet-like boot struck the ball with an unearthly thud. The ball boomed towards the uprights, turning end-for-end. The crowd watched with amusement at first, waiting for the ball to eventually fall short of its mark. But the ball kept climbing and climbing towards the goalpost.

Within moments, it became apparent that Dempsey's improbable kick just might have a chance. Now the crowd watched breathlessly as the ball streaked for the goalpost. Just when the ball appeared to have lost its steam, it flew over the crossbar. The referee raised his hands, and Dempsey entered NFL history books for kicking the league's longest field goal. Even more, the field goal won the game. Dempsey was carried off the field by his elated teammates as the home crowd cheered wildly.

New Orleans Saints' Tom Dempsey (19), who is missing a hand and part of his right foot, kicks a record-setting 63-yard field goal to beat the Lions with only two seconds remaining in the game.

Archie Manning

Though the Saints were exciting to watch, they had losing seasons from 1967 to 1970. In January 1971, the Saints received their first number-one draft pick. Hoping to build their team into a champion, they chose quarterback Archie Manning from the University of Mississippi.

Archie Manning was the Saints franchise player in the 1970s.

Manning was the starting quarterback in the season opener against the Los Angeles Rams. Although the Rams' defense pressured Manning throughout the game, the rookie quarterback passed for one touchdown and ran for another, leading his team to an impressive win.

Manning could do it all. He had a strong, accurate arm and could scramble and run with the ball. But in 1976, he missed the entire season because of tendinitis.

After two operations, Manning successfully returned to the game. In his 11-year career with New Orleans, Manning set game, season, and career passing records.

Archie Manning running with the ball against the 49ers.

The Coaches

Head coaches Hank Stram (1976-1977) and Dick Nolan (1978-1980) were in charge of surrounding Manning with talented players. Stram had 15 years of experience and 129 career victories to his credit. Even more, he had coached the American Football Conference's (AFC's) Kansas City Chiefs to a Super Bowl victory in 1970. Nolan had led the San Francisco 49ers to three NFC Western Division championships.

Both coaches found the talented young players the Saints needed. Chuck Muncie was the Saints' first-round draft pick in 1976. He was joined by running back Tony Galbreath, who also became a leading receiver. The Saints powerful running attack and their tough defensive line earned them an 8-8 record in 1979—good for a second place finish. But the Saints were not happy with second place. They felt they were a better team, and dedicated the following season to prove their point.

Manning could do it all, and make it look so easy.

Bum Phillips

In 1980, however, the Saints did an about-face, and finished with a team-worst 1-15 record. The players were stunned and the fans booed loudly. No one looked forward to the next season—except for the new head coach.

O. A. Phillips, better known as "Bum," joined the Saints in 1981. He brought a winning attitude to the struggling Saints. Phillips had coached the AFC's Houston Oilers to three successive AFC playoffs.

**Saints running back Chuck Muncie
breaks a tackle against Tampa Bay.**

Phillips was a colorful character. He walked the sidelines dressed in lizard skin cowboy boots, blue jeans, a plaid western shirt, and his famous Stetson cowboy hat. His knowledge of the game, and his sense of humor, soon won him many fans—including his players. Suddenly, the Saints felt they could win again.

Because of his reputation, Phillips lured many talented players to New Orleans—two of whom starred on Phillips's former team. Kenny "The Snake" Stabler, the Oilers' leading passer in 1980 and 1981, came to New Orleans as a backup for Archie Manning. When Manning objected to Stabler's presence, Phillips traded Manning to Houston for Oilers' tackle Leon Gray.

Now the starting quarterback, Stabler led the Saints' offense for three seasons until he retired in 1984. Former New York Jets quarterback Richard Todd came to New Orleans in 1984 to take Stabler's place.

Another former Oiler, Earl Campbell, came to New Orleans for the 1984 and 1985 seasons. Campbell was one of the NFL's all-time leading rushers and brought excitement—and fans—back to the SuperDome.

Phillips also rebuilt the Saints through the college draft. George Rogers, 1980 Heisman Trophy winner, was New Orleans' first-round draft pick in 1981. Rogers went on to set Saints career, single-season, and single-game rushing records.

Bum Phillips built a new and improved Saints team.

New Orleans Saints

Tom Dempsey holds the NFL record for the longest field goal in 1970.

20

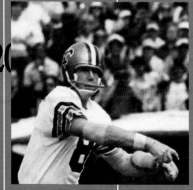

40

Quarterback Archie Manning, was drafted by the Saints in 1971.

New O
Sa

In 1967, Tom Fears, the first head coach of the Saints.

10   20

40

First ever quarterback of the Saints, Billy Kilmer, 1967.

0   20   10

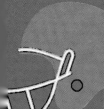

Running back Chuck Muncie,
first round pick in 1976.

Quarterback Bobby Hebert, was
acquired by the Saints in 1986.

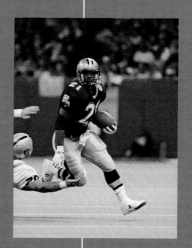

Kicker Morten
Andersen, 1990.

Running back
Dalton Hilliard,
1990.

40   30   20   10

Rebuilding

Despite the new talent, the Saints continued to struggle. New Orleans businessman Tom Benson bought the team in May 1985, but a disappointing 5-11 record brought more changes. Bum Phillips resigned, Earl Campbell retired, and George Rogers was traded to Washington.

Benson did not stop his rebuilding efforts with the players. He hired Jim Finks as president and general manager in 1986. With a 37-year career in sports as a player, coach, and administrator, Finks gave New Orleans the steady leadership they needed. He had spent 10 years with the Minnesota Vikings and saw them reach the Super Bowl twice. In 1974, Finks left the Vikings for the Chicago Bears, then went to work for baseball's Chicago Cubs.

The Saints also hired Jim Mora as head coach. Mora was the first Saints' coach to earn more wins than losses. As head coach of the Philadelphia/Baltimore Stars of the USFL, Mora racked up an amazing 48-13-1 record.

Mora's first season ended with an improved 7-9 record. But Mora was not satisfied. He was used to winning, and would not accept anything but excellence.

The Saints responded with winning seasons in 1987, 1988, and 1989. But Mora wouldn't rest until the Saints were the NFL's best team.

Morten Andersen

The Saints owed their turnaround to young players that Mora had developed. One of them was Morten Andersen, one of the NFL's most accurate kickers.

Andersen was born in Denmark. He had never kicked a football until coming to the United States as a 17-year-old exchange student. But when it came to other sports, Andersen was a fanatic. He liked swimming, running, skiing, cycling, and tennis. He also lifted weights five days a week.

Andersen eventually played football for Michigan State University. After graduating, he joined the Saints. He went on to establish many Saints scoring records.

Another star player was center Joel Hilgenberg. He came from a family with a rich football tradition. Hilgenberg's father, Jerry, was an All-American center at the University of Iowa. Brothers Jim and Jay also played for Iowa, and uncle Wally was a Minnesota Vikings' star.

Hilgenberg blocked for one of New Orleans' most successful runners, Dalton Hilliard. A graduate of Louisiana State University, Hilliard ranked third behind Herschel Walker and Bo Jackson in career rushing yardage in the Southeastern Conference (SEC). Hilliard could do everything—including rush, receive, and return kickoffs. He led the Saints in rushing in 1988 and 1989.

The heart of Mora's attack was Louisiana native Bobby Hebert. He had a strong, accurate throwing arm. Hebert came to New Orleans after three seasons with the USFL's Michigan Panthers. In 1983, Hebert defeated Jim Mora's Philadelphia Stars in the USFL's first championship game. Two years later, Hebert, playing for the Oakland Invaders, lost to Mora's Baltimore Stars in another USFL championship game. When the USFL folded, Hebert signed with the Saints.

Hebert got off to a rocky start in the NFL. He suffered a broken foot in 1986 and played six games in 1987 with a swollen knee. But in 1988, Hebert had his best year ever.

Hebert could not avoid his injury problems. In a 1989 game against Tampa Bay, Buccaneers safety Mark Robinson kneed Hebert. The Saints' quarterback suffered his eighth career concussion and lost two front teeth.

Morten Andersen is one of the NFL's most accurate kickers.

The 1990s

The Saints spent the 1990 season trying to get to .500, a mark they achieved with two straight wins at the end. Hebert spent the season holding out, and John Fourcade got the job. But after three games, general manager Jim Finks mortgaged the future by sending three high draft picks to Dallas for Steve Walsh. Although the team had a winning record with Walsh at the helm, his play was inconsistent. The strength of the team remained with the defense, especially with the linebackers. New Orleans made the playoffs, but were bounced 16-6 by the Bears in Chicago.

Management knew that Hebert was the heart and soul of the team, and they made sure he was signed in 1991. For the first time in their 15-year history, the Saints won a division championship with an 11-5 record. Hebert led the Saints to a 9-2 record. Walsh had to finish the season when Hebert got injured.

Floyd Turner blossomed into a fine wide receiver, scoring eight touchdowns. But the running attack was nonexistent, with nobody gaining 500 yards. Defense was still the team's strength. They led the NFL with fewest points allowed. Linebacker Pat Swilling led the NFL in sacks and was voted the league's Defensive Player of the Year.

Optimism ran high for the playoffs. The Saints entertained the Atlanta Falcons in the first round. New Orleans jumped out to a 7-0 first-quarter lead when Hebert found Turner with a 26-yard scoring strike. Andersen tacked on two second-quarter field goals as the Saints took a 13-10 lead into halftime. But the Falcons grabbed a 17-13 lead in the third quarter.

Dalton Hilliard's 1-yard run in the fourth quarter put the Saints ahead 21-17. But after that it was all Atlanta as they scored 10 unanswered points for a 27-20 upset win. The Saints knew they had the talent to go to the Super Bowl. But they would have to play better in the playoffs if they wanted to win it all.

In 1992, the 12-4 Saints nearly won their division again. But they couldn't beat the San Francisco 49ers. The Saints sent an unprecedented four linebackers to the Pro Bowl—Rickey Jackson, Vaughn Johnson, Sam Mills, and Pat Swilling—and end Wayne Martin emerged as a pass-rushing force.

But the offense remained average. When hot, Hebert formed a dangerous combination with Eric Martin (68 catches, 5 touchdowns). But for the most part, coach Jim Mora's troops relied on a ground game that was anything but effective. Rookie Vaughn Dunbar led the team with only 565 yards rushing, but he lost his starting job by midseason. The only real bright spot was the kicking game. Morten Andersen tied for the NFC lead with 120 points.

Despite the second-place finish, the Saints still had one of the best teams in the NFL. They began the playoffs at home against the Philadelphia Eagles. New Orleans opened the scoring on a 1-yard touchdown run by Heyward and slowly built a 17-7 halftime lead. The Saints and Eagles traded field goals in the third quarter and it looked like New Orleans would hang on for the win. After all, they had one of the league's best defenses.

But disaster struck in the fourth quarter. Philadelphia scored two quick touchdowns, then added a safety and a field goal for a commanding 29-20 lead. An 18-yard interception for a touchdown iced the game for the Eagles as they won 36-20.

Management was clearly disappointed in the outcome and decided to shake up the team. They brought in Wade Wilson from the Vikings to replace Hebert. At first Wilson played well as the Saints jumped out to a 5-0 record. But then they lost 6 of 8 games as Wilson threw 14 interceptions in the final 11 games. The Saints finished with an 8-8 mark and out of the playoffs.

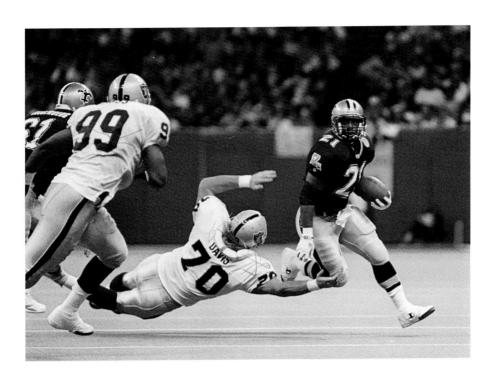

One of the Saints most successful runners was Dalton Hilliard.

The Saints collapse was due in part to the aging defense which suffered key injuries. They finished 22nd in points allowed. The only bright spots were running back Derek Brown (705 yards rushing) and linebacker Renaldo Turnbull, who tied for the NFC lead with 13 sacks.

The Saints seemed to be at the crossroads as the 1994 season began. No one knew if they would get better or worse. An opening-day 30-17 loss to the Kansas City Chiefs set the tone for the season. By Week 6, the Saints were 2-4 and in last place in the NFC West.

The season's highlight came in Week 8 against the Los Angeles Rams. Tyrone Hughes tied an NFL game record by returning two kickoffs (92 and 98 yards) for touchdowns. He also set one-game records for most kickoff-return yards (304) and most combined kick-return yards (347). Even better, the Saints won the game 37-34.

Quarterback Bobby Hebert shakes off a tackle by Los Angeles Rams linebacker Kevin Greene.

By Week 12, the Saints had fallen to 4-7 and were tied with the Rams for last place. In a Week 14 showdown with L.A., the Saints took charge of the game and won easily 31-15, vaulting themselves into third place with a 5-8 record. The following week, the Saints defeated Atlanta 29-20 to tie the Falcons for second place. In the final week of the season, New Orleans won a shootout with the Denver Broncos to clinch second place with a 7-9 record. It was not, however, good enough to make the playoffs.

§

In the past, New Orleans had been on top of their game with punishing defenses and a skilled aerial attack run by a top-notch quarterback. With Hebert gone and their defensive corps depleted, the New Orleans Saints have entered a rebuilding stage. They know the formula for success. If they should find the right combination of players, the Saints will go marching back to the top of the NFC West.

GLOSSARY

ALL-PRO—A player who is voted to the Pro Bowl.

BACKFIELD—Players whose position is behind the line of scrimmage.

CORNERBACK—Either of two defensive halfbacks stationed a short distance behind the linebackers and relatively near the sidelines.

DEFENSIVE END—A defensive player who plays on the end of the line and often next to the defensive tackle.

DEFENSIVE TACKLE—A defensive player who plays on the line and between the guard and end.

ELIGIBLE—A player who is qualified to be voted into the Hall of Fame.

END ZONE—The area on either end of a football field where players score touchdowns.

EXTRA POINT—The additional one-point score added after a player makes a touchdown. Teams earn extra points if the placekicker kicks the ball through the uprights of the goalpost, or if an offensive player crosses the goal line with the football before being tackled.

FIELD GOAL—A three-point score awarded when a placekicker kicks the ball through the uprights of the goalpost.

FULLBACK—An offensive player who often lines up farthest behind the front line.

FUMBLE—When a player loses control of the football.

GUARD—An offensive lineman who plays between the tackles and center.

GROUND GAME—The running game.

HALFBACK—An offensive player whose position is behind the line of scrimmage.

HALFTIME—The time period between the second and third quarters of a football game.

INTERCEPTION—When a defensive player catches a pass from an offensive player.

KICK RETURNER—An offensive player who returns kickoffs.

LINEBACKER—A defensive player whose position is behind the line of scrimmage.

LINEMAN—An offensive or defensive player who plays on the line of scrimmage.

PASS—To throw the ball.

PASS RECEIVER—An offensive player who runs pass routes and catches passes.

PLACEKICKER—An offensive player who kicks extra points and field goals. The placekicker also kicks the ball from a tee to the opponent after his team has scored.

PLAYOFFS—The postseason games played amongst the division winners and wild card teams which determines the Super Bowl champion.

PRO BOWL—The postseason All-Star game which showcases the NFL's best players.

PUNT—To kick the ball to the opponent.

QUARTER—One of four 15-minute time periods that makes up a football game.

QUARTERBACK—The backfield player who usually calls the signals for the plays.

REGULAR SEASON—The games played after the preseason and before the playoffs.

ROOKIE—A first-year player.

RUNNING BACK—A backfield player who usually runs with the ball.

RUSH—To run with the football.

SACK—To tackle the quarterback behind the line of scrimmage.

SAFETY—A defensive back who plays behind the linemen and linebackers. Also, two points awarded for tackling an offensive player in his own end zone when he's carrying the ball.

SPECIAL TEAMS—Squads of football players that perform special tasks (for example, kickoff team and punt-return team).

SPONSOR—A person or company that finances a football team.

SUPER BOWL—The NFL championship game played between the AFC champion and the NFC champion.

T FORMATION—An offensive formation in which the fullback lines up behind the center and quarterback with one halfback stationed on each side of the fullback.

TACKLE—An offensive or defensive lineman who plays between the ends and the guards.

TAILBACK—The offensive back farthest from the line of scrimmage.

TIGHT END—An offensive lineman who is stationed next to the tackles, and who usually blocks or catches passes.

TOUCHDOWN—When one team crosses the goal line of the other team's end zone. A touchdown is worth six points.

TURNOVER—To turn the ball over to an opponent either by a fumble, an interception, or on downs.

UNDERDOG—The team that is picked to lose the game.

WIDE RECEIVER—An offensive player who is stationed relatively close to the sidelines and who usually catches passes.

WILD CARD—A team that makes the playoffs without winning its division.

ZONE PASS DEFENSE—A pass defense method where defensive backs defend a certain area of the playing field rather than individual pass receivers.

INDEX